My Grand Adventure

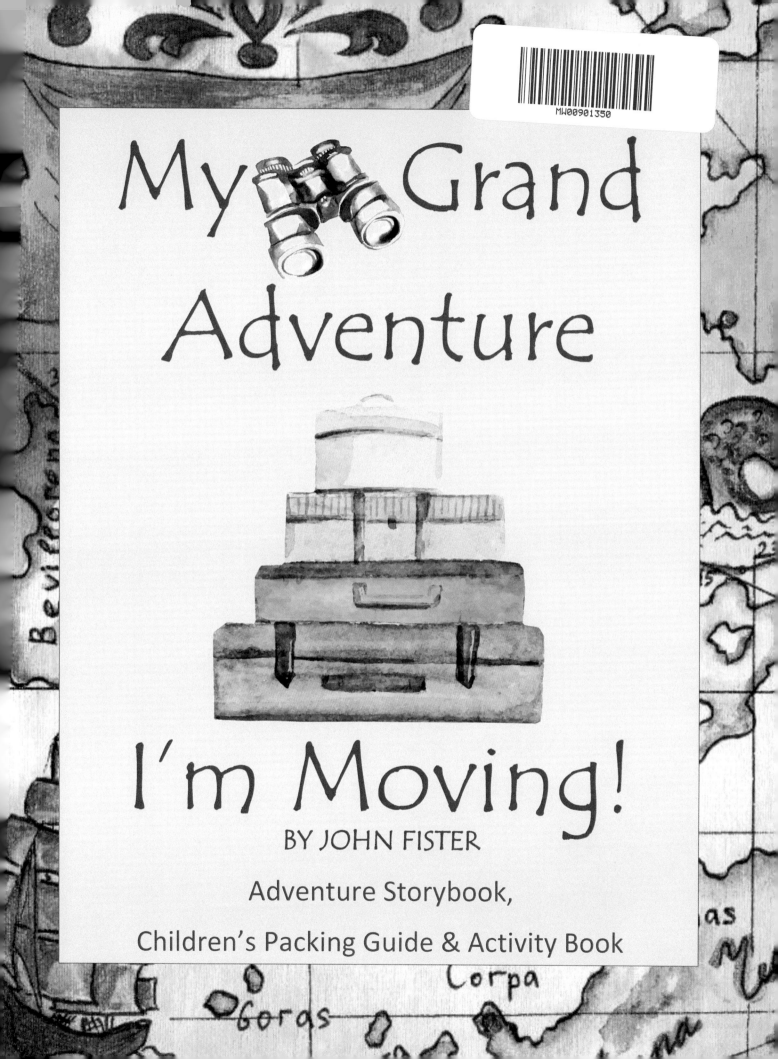

I'm Moving!

BY JOHN FISTER

Adventure Storybook,

Children's Packing Guide & Activity Book

I know there is a grand adventure ahead of me. The location is a bit of a mystery but I have been told the name of the city and state. Research is my favorite thing. I am going to scout out the land, the territory. I've collected all the right equipment – binoculars, scope, compass and maps. Now it's time to get the facts!

Our maps are hard to read. I got them out of the attic. We will employ the use of the compass to locate my new city and state. We must use the compass rose – it tells us in which direction we will travel. There is a treasure map in this book. It is nowhere near my new city but it sure is fun!

Create your own treasure island map

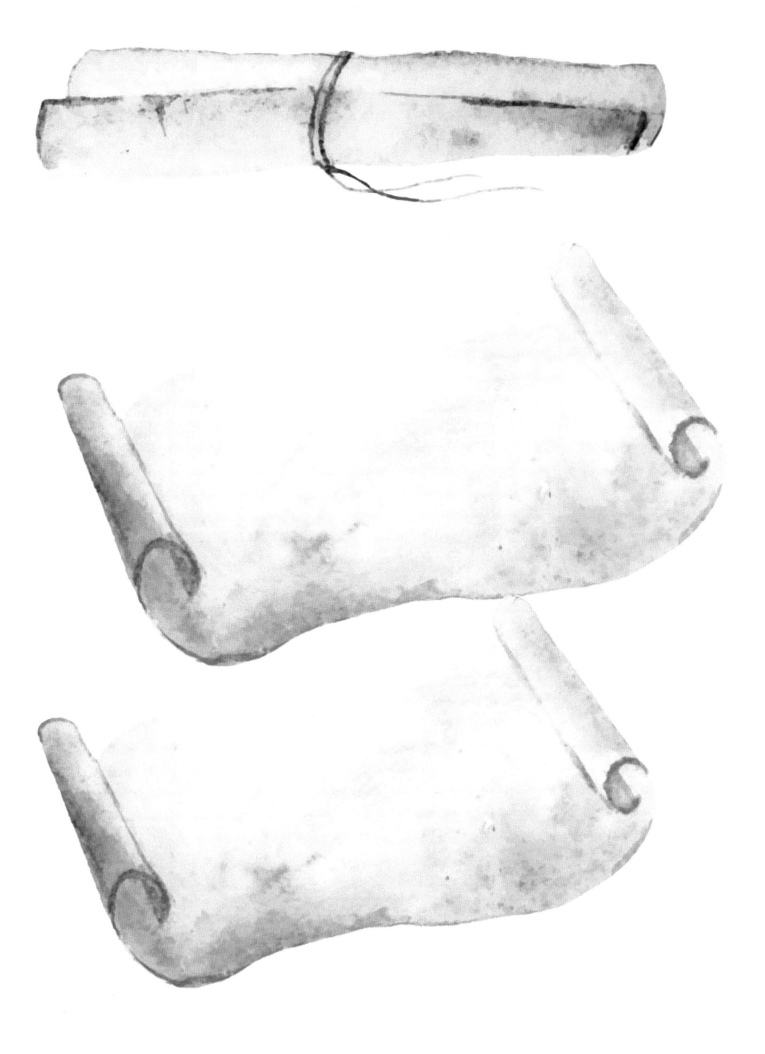

There is a lot of moving going on around the world. My mom told me thousands of families will move to a new city this summer. That means there must be 10 thousand kids moving to new cities. Well, I certainly won't be the only new kid in my new neighborhood. That's a lot of suitcases being packed with favorite clothes and favorite toys.

Locating my new city is important. It will help me determine if we will travel by land, sea or sky to reach our new home. After all, I would like to know if my expression will be "AHOY MATIE," or "ONWARD AND UPWARD."

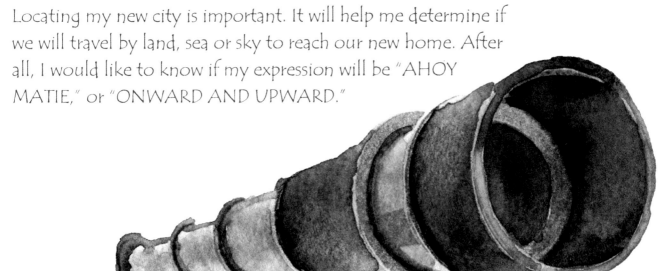

No matter where our new city is, no matter which direction I will go, I am ready for my grand adventure to begin!

Your grand adventure will not occur on a treasure map but a state map or map of the United States. Your adventure will be a vivid, fun and colorful adventure that will include traveling across parts of the United States.

Circle 10 of your favorite things in this picture!

What is your new address?

There will be lots of packing, lots of boxes and most certainly a TRUCK to move all of your belongings. Your couch, your chairs, your bed, everything you own will go into this truck and be delivered to your new home! Nothing will be left behind!

There will be organizing…

There will be labeling…

And there will be resting.

Which toys will you pack and which ones can you take with you in your suitcase?

Ask your parents to use clear bins instead of boxes for your FAVORITE toys so you can find them easily when you get to your new home.

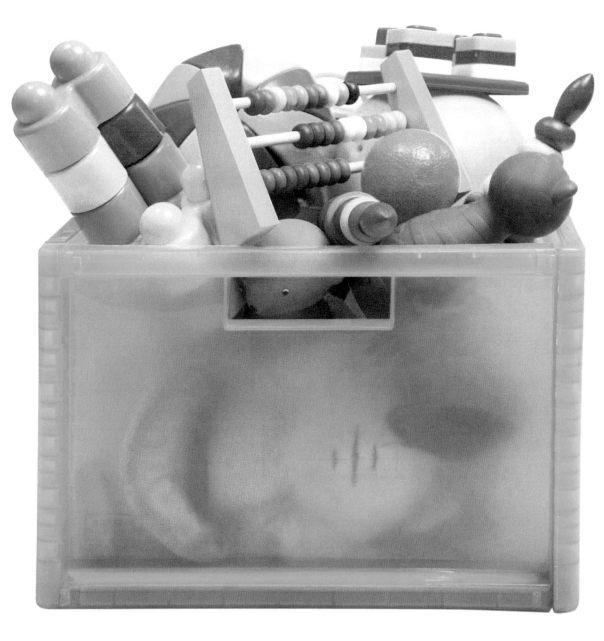

Can you pack these bins? Draw the toys inside
the bin or draw a line from the toy to the bin.

List your favorite toys here:

_____

_____

_____

_____

Can you draw some in these bins?

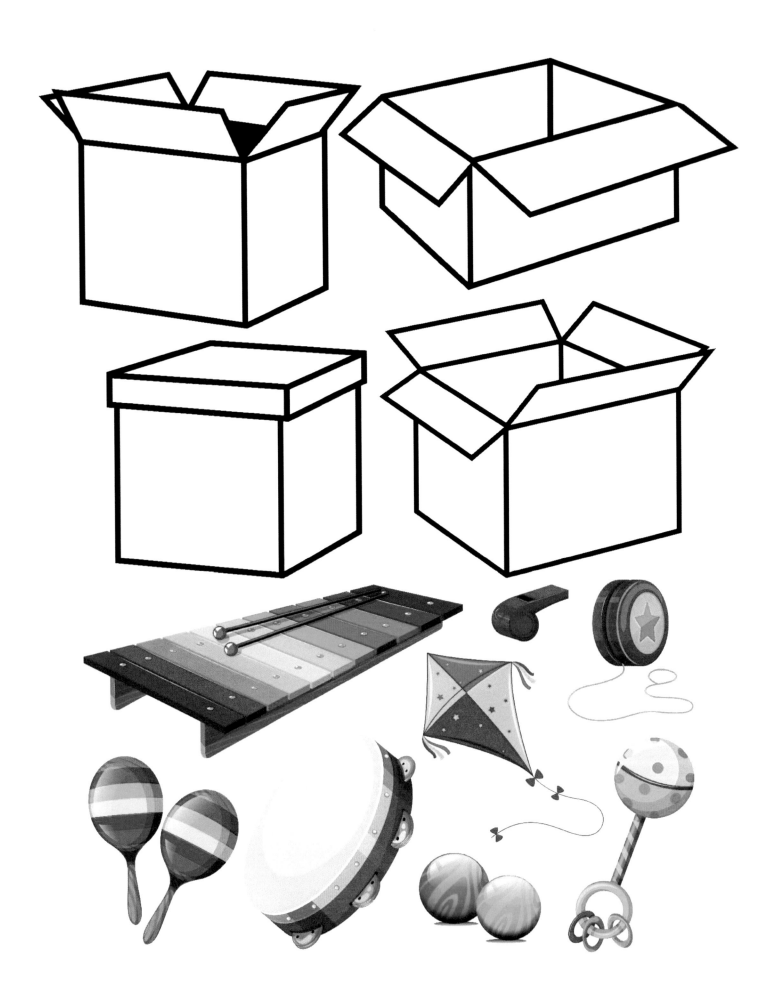

Let's pack other toys in boxes
and seal the boxes with tape.
Label the boxes with your name.

After all the boxes have been packed and sealed, your boxes will be carried to and loaded onto the truck. It will take about one day to complete this task.

Can you color the "Carrier Process"?

Which vehicles will your family use to move?

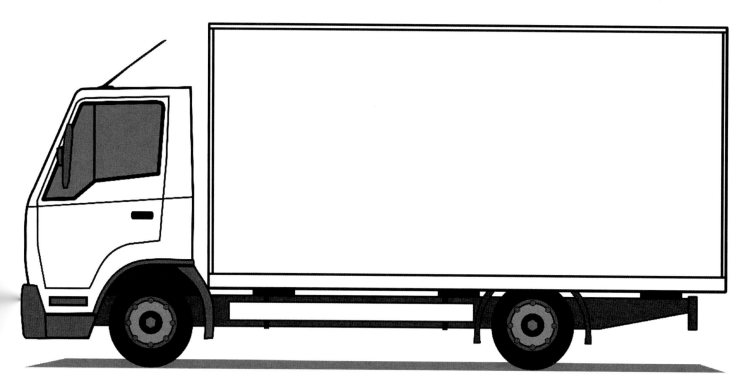

Fill this truck with furniture.

Fill this truck with boxes.

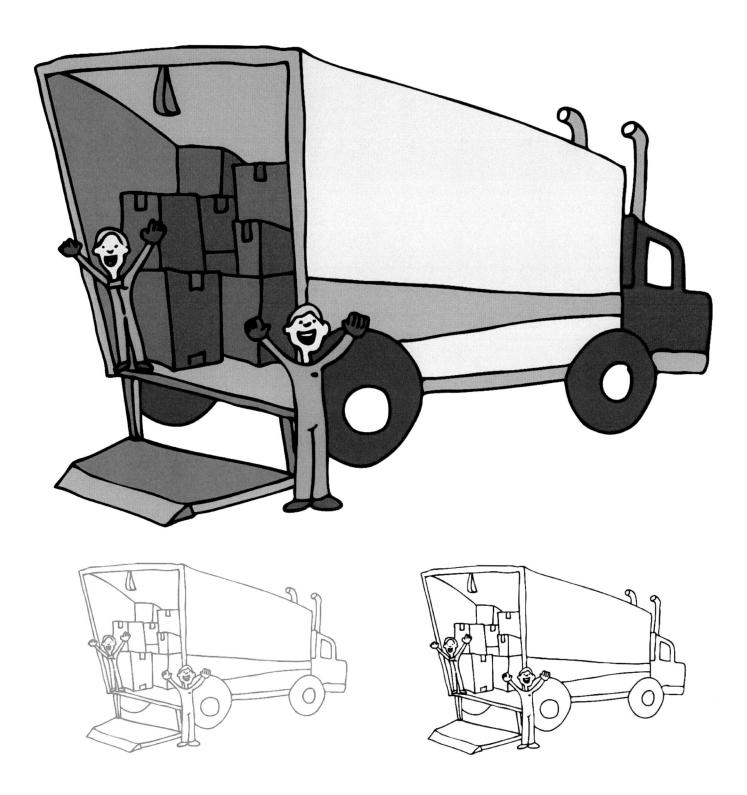

This is what moving day looked like in the olden days. Today, it looks like this...

The truck is loaded and the driver gets on the highway to drive to your new house. Can you write your family's name on the side of this truck?

Can you write the name of the moving company on the truck above? Draw the driver and the driver's helper in the cab of this big rig.

While your truck is driving to your new house, you will be driving or flying there, too! Who will arrive first?

What city and state do you live in now?

_____

To which city and state are you moving?

_____

Your new home will be exciting and different. Family members will pick their favorite rooms. Your pets will be so excited for the new adventure! You will be able to decorate your new room and experience a fun new setup.

It will feel like home once you unpack all your belongings. Your furniture will feel cozy once again. There will be a lot to explore in your new home, your new neighborhood and new town. Your parents will help you join clubs and activities that you enjoy and register you for school and you will begin to make new friends. You will have your old friends AND your new friends!

HOME sweet HOME

There will be a moment when you will remember the adventure you had. Once you are unpacked, settled in and playing again with all your favorite things, you will realize you did have a GRAND ADVENTURE. You experienced something adventurous and exciting like nothing you have experienced before. And there is still a great adventure ahead of you. So get out your compass and your maps and get ready for the wonder of it all!

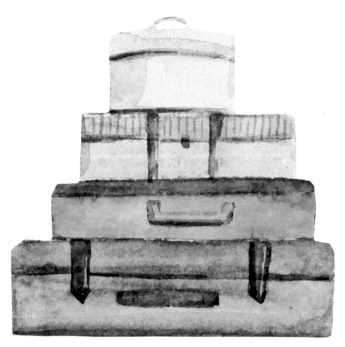

33
30
28
28 Rocca

28 27
acunda

Los Indiana

Salomon

Cor

Goras

ora

About the Author

John Fister is a third generation, 35-year, award winning veteran of the moving and storage industry. He has enjoyed all aspects of the business over the years. From management and sales, to owning and operating his own moving van. Being a van operator and physically being involved in each move is by far his favorite aspect of the business.

"Relocating as an individual or as a family can be very stressful. My goal on every move is to make it a pleasant and stress-free experience and to exceed our customers' expectations."

Fister's grandfather, Vincent Fister, Sr. of Lexington, Kentucky began a family owned moving and storage business – Vincent Fister, Inc. Moving & Storage - that has stayed in the family and continues today. Fister's father, Vincent Fister, Jr. continued the tradition, owning several moving and storage businesses across the United States.

This moving adventure book is a handbook and an activity book, containing activities for children of all ages. Each child can become engaged in the moving process and feel he/she, too, can be in charge of his/her destiny! These activities provide parents with insight into the ideal packing process for children's belongings, relocation and destination activities, as well as assurance that everything will come together at the other end of the move. Enjoy your adventure!

Vincent Fister, Sr., Founder of Vincent Fister, Inc. Moving & Storage, and three of his grandchildren: Nancy, John and Renee.